# JOSH GROSS

# THE LAST WORD

Josh Gross, whose first word was "Rosebud," attended Beverly Hills High School and is now a sophomore at the University of California at Berkeley.

# THE LAST WORD

# THE LAST WORD

*Final Scenes from Favorite Motion Pictures*

## JOSH GROSS

VINTAGE BOOKS

A DIVISION OF RANDOM HOUSE, INC.

NEW YORK

A VINTAGE ORIGINAL, DECEMBER 1992
FIRST EDITION

Library of Congress Cataloging-in-Publication Data
Gross, Josh.
The last word / Josh Gross.
p.   cm.
ISBN 0-679-73390-6
1. Motion picture plays—United States—History and criticism.
2. Closure (Rhetoric)   I. Title.
PN1995.G6896   1992
791.43′75′0973—dc20         91-50728
CIP

Book design by JoAnne Metsch

Author photo copyright © 1992 by Gila Lane

Manufactured in the United States of America

10   9   8   7   6   5   4   3   2   1

TO
JOAN and JACK GROSS
and
PETER STONE

For their advice and support

# ACKNOWLEDGMENTS

I am grateful to the following people for their invaluable assistance with this project:

The staff of the Academy of Motion Pictures-Arts and Sciences; Martin Asher; Dan Aykroyd; Judith Jacklin Belushi; Peter Benchley; Shirley Bernstein; Paul Bloch; Jacob Bloom; Marshall Brickman; Bernie Brillstein; Paula Broussard; Diana Brown; Carol Bua; Philip Buchbinder; Cherise Carroll; Patricia Cherone; Norma Lee Clark; Bari Cohen; Nancy Cushing-Jones; Mrs. I.A.L. Diamond; Robin Desser; Phil Gersh; Carl Gottlieb; Lew Grimes; Larry Grossman; Bill Haber; Caitlin Hamilton; Irene Hayman; Albert Heit; Alan Hergott; Evelyn Hunter; Diane Isaacs; Morton Janklow; Joan Kan; Alex Karasik; Rick Kurshner; Edward Kastenmeier; John Landis; Peter Langs; Robert Lantz; Ernest Lehman; Martha Luttrell; Melissa Mathison; Larry McCallister; Ilene Miller; Kevin Mills; Bruce Moccia; Julia Phillips; Joan Pierce; Peter Raleigh; Michael Reagan; Stephen Rodgers; Scott Rosen; June Shelley; Robert Sieber; Stirling Silliphant; Stephany Simon; Hillarie Singer; Marsinay Smith; Stephen Sondheim; Rosalie Swedlin; Victoria Traube; Mike Voss; Sally Willcox; Billy Wilder; Donetta Wilson; Carole Henderson Wright; Tonie Zwaneveld.

# CONTENTS

# INTRODUCTION

Shocking, heart-rending, captivating, surprising, but *always* memorable—such should be the final scene of a great movie, a finale that leaves the viewer with an indescribable feeling that somehow encapsulates the messages and themes of the film he or she has just watched. A movie's last scene is, of course, the final opportunity a filmmaker has to get his point across and, as such, it is often the most powerful and unforgettable part of a movie. (On the other hand, how many of us have cringed at the sappy, pat, or just disappointing finale of a film we were enjoying up to that point?)

Because I've always loved the endings of movies, at the age of twelve I began to compile my personal list of favorites. Like any movie fan, I had seen certain films so many times that I could recite portions of them verbatim. But when I would quiz people about their knowledge of a given film, it was always the last scene that would elicit huge smiles, perfectly accented imitations, or, on some occasions, goose bumps and tears.

Strangely, the endings of certain movies get distorted by people over time. Many of my friends still insist that the last line of *Gone With the Wind* is "Frankly, my dear, I don't give a damn." Please note, however, that *The Last Word* should not be used to decide wagers!

My research for this book was done primarily at the Academy of Motion Picture Arts and Sciences, which should be commended for establishing the definitive archive for American film in this country. I am particularly grateful to the Academy Library staff, for without their knowledge and patience this book could not have been completed.

My project, however, did not end with merely transcribing the screenplays as I found them. After I had submitted my manuscript, I learned that I had to track down the copyright holder of every film included in this book and obtain a legal release to use the collected excerpts. Although this was sometimes a grueling task, it spawned some truly amusing stories, and more often than not proved to be more surprising than tedious. Countless estates have changed hands, and many films have been sold since their original release, which created a maze of paperwork and phone calls that frequently led me to unusual places. Sometimes my requests were altogether ignored; after all, as many reasoned, who had time for a teenager's book project when there were multi-million dollar contracts to be negotiated? Luckily, I found enough amenable people—at literally every level of the corporate ladder—to allow this collection to go to press.

My list of films has changed somewhat over the last six years, but I truly feel it is an accurate representation of the kinds of motion pictures I wanted to include when I started the project. One should note that this book does not consist of the final scenes of the most critically acclaimed films, or the biggest box office hits of all time. It is instead eclectic, ranging from the original *Jazz Singer* to the recent *Untouchables,* representing along the way such lesser-known gems as *Dr. Ehrlich's Magic Bullet* and *The President's Analyst.* (I entirely agree with Leonard Maltin, who called the latter's ending "a beauty.") Naturally everyone has his or her personal favorite endings, and some will be perplexed that my selections aren't theirs. But for the most part, I think that there is no question that this book represents some of the high points of filmmaking over the past seventy years.

The stills adjacent to the text are designed to visually set the stage for the endings. I have tried to include shots that are as close to the ending as possible, but in some cases they simply were not available. In these instances I selected stills that best captured the flavor of the movie as a whole. When applicable I have also included the original titles of certain screenplays in smaller type, as well as ⊺ for films, actors, screenwriters, etc., that were awarded Oscars.

My last step in preparing *The Last Word* was to watch the ending of every film once again for accuracy. Because motion pictures are changed, either by ad libs on the set or by editors on the cutting room floor, I found that the shooting script I transcribed was often not the same as the film that was subsequently released. I made a substantial number of revisions in an attempt both to preserve the language of the screenwriter and to present what was actually shown on the screen.

The collection you see before you is an exhilarating replication of some of the best endings in motion picture history. Our movies remain among our most valuable exports; may we remain confident that we can in the next seventy years produce another sixty movies as beloved as the films that follow.

*Josh Gross*
*Beverly Hills, California*
*December 1992*

# THE LAST WORD

# ADAM'S RIB · 1949

**STARRING:**

SPENCER TRACY / KATHARINE HEPBURN / JUDY HOLLIDAY
TOM EWELL / DAVID WAYNE

*M - G - M*

Screenplay by: GARSON KANIN and RUTH GORDON
Produced by: LAURENCE WEINGARTEN
Directed by: GEORGE CUKOR

INTERIOR: BEDROOM

> **AMANDA** (KATHARINE HEPBURN)
> Shows what I say is true. No difference between the sexes. None. Men. Women. The same.

> **ADAM** (SPENCER TRACY)
> They are, huh?

> **AMANDA**
> Well, maybe there is a difference. But it's a *little* difference.

> **ADAM**
> Yeah? Well, as the French say . . .

> **AMANDA**
> What do they say?

> **ADAM**
> *Vive la différence.*

> **AMANDA**
> Which means . . . ?

> **ADAM**
> Which means, hooray for that little difference.

# THE AFRICAN QUEEN · 1951

**STARRING:**

KATHARINE HEPBURN / HUMPHREY BOGART / ROBERT
MORLEY
PETER BULL / THEODORE BIKEL

*Romulus / Horizon Pictures*

*United Artists Release*

Screenplay by: JAMES AGEE*
Produced by: SAM SPIEGEL
Directed by: JOHN HUSTON
*Based on the novel by C. S. Forester.*

EXTERIOR: IN THE WATER – DAY

> **ALLNUTT** (HUMPHREY BOGART)
> Wot 'appened?

> **ROSE** (KATHARINE HEPBURN)
> We did it, Charlie, we did it!

> **ALLNUTT**
> But 'ow?

*Rose holds a piece of wreckage that shows the name* African Queen, *which is floating in the water.*

> **ALLNUTT**
> Well, what do you think . . . you all right, Mrs. Allnutt?

> **ROSE**
> Wonderful, simply wonderful. And you, Mr. Allnutt?

> **ALLNUTT**
> Pretty good . . . for an old married man!

> **ROSE**
> I'm all twisted around, Charlie, which way is the east shore?

> **ALLNUTT**
> The way we're swimming toward, old girl.

*The two begin to swim to shore, singing "There was an old fisherman . . ." as the music swells.*

# AIRPLANE! · 1980

**STARRING:**
ROBERT HAYS / JULIE HAGERTY / ROBERT STACK
LLOYD BRIDGES / PETER GRAVES

*Paramount*

Screenplay by: JIM ABRAHAMS, DAVID ZUCKER, JERRY ZUCKER
Produced by: JAN DAVISON
Directed by: JIM ABRAHAMS, DAVID ZUCKER, JERRY ZUCKER

EXTERIOR: AIRFIELD – NIGHT

*Ted* (ROBERT HAYS) *and Elaine* (JULIE HAGERTY) *are alone on the runway. Behind them is flight 209. They kiss passionately. The music swells.*

*We see a grimace on Elaine's face. Suddenly, the engines rev up. Astonished, they look up into the cockpit and see that the automatic pilot is at the controls. He salutes Ted and Elaine and winks at the camera. They wave back. Beside him a female automatic pilot is inflated.*

*The plane takes off as sky rockets and fireworks illuminate the night sky.*

# ALL ABOUT EVE · 1950 ▼

**STARRING:**
BETTE DAVIS / ANNE BAXTER / GEORGE SANDERS ❙
CELESTE HOLM / GARY MERRILL

*20th Century-Fox*

Screenplay by: JOSEPH L. MANKIEWICZ ❙
Produced by: DARYL F. ZANUCK
Directed by: JOSEPH L. MANKIEWICZ ❙

INTERIOR: ROOM

> **EVE** (ANNE BAXTER)
> *(offscreen, sleepy, calling from the living room)*
> Who was it?

> **PHOEBE** (BARBARA BATES)
> Just a taxi driver, Miss Harrington. You left the award in his cab and he brought it back.

> **EVE**
> *(offscreen)*
> Oh. Put it on one of the trunks, will you? I want to pack it . . .

> **PHOEBE**
> Sure, Miss Harrington.

*Phoebe takes the award into the bedroom and sets it on a trunk. As she starts out, she sees Eve's wrap on the bed. She listens, then, quietly puts on the wrap and picks up the award.*

*Slowly, Phoebe walks to a large four-mirrored cheval. With grave and infinite dignity she holds the award to her, and bows, again and again and again—as if to the applause of a multitude.*

# ANNIE HALL · (ANHEDONIA) · 1977 ▼

**STARRING:**

WOODY ALLEN / DIANE KEATON ❗/ TONY ROBERTS
PAUL SIMON / SHELLEY DUVALL

*United Artists*

Screenplay by: WOODY ALLEN ❗ and MARSHALL BRICKMAN ❗
Produced by: JACK ROLLINS and CHARLES H. JOFFE
Directed by: WOODY ALLEN ❗

EXTERIOR: A NEW YORK STREET – DAY

*Alvy Singer* (WOODY ALLEN) *and Annie Hall* (DIANE KEATON) *are seen shaking hands and parting in the distance.*

**ALVY**
. . . It was great seeing Annie again and I
realized what a terrific person she was and how
much fun it was knowing her and I thought of
that old joke, you know, this, this, this guy goes
to a psychiatrist and says, Doc, uh, my brother's
crazy, he thinks he's a chicken and, uh, the
doctor says, well why don't you turn him in? And
the guy says, I would, but I need the eggs. Well, I
guess that's pretty much how I feel about
relationships. You know, they're totally irrational
and crazy and absurd and, but uh, I guess we
keep going through it . . . because . . . most of
us need the eggs.

EXTERIOR: A NEW YORK STREET

*From the window of O'Neal's restaurant, we see the street corner is now deserted and empty. Alvy and Annie have gone their separate ways.*

# THE APARTMENT · 1960 ▼

**STARRING:**
JACK LEMMON / SHIRLEY MacLAINE / FRED MacMURRAY
RAY WALSTON / JACK KRUSCHEN

*United Artists*

Screenplay by: BILLY WILDER ❚ and I.A.L. DIAMOND ❚
Produced by: BILLY WILDER
Directed by: BILLY WILDER ❚

INTERIOR: THE APARTMENT – NIGHT

*Fran* (SHIRLEY MACLAINE) *and Bud* (JACK LEMMON) *sit opposite each other on the couch in Bud's apartment.*

> **BUD**
> *(cutting a card)*
> I love you, Miss Kubelik.

> **FRAN**
> *(cutting a card)*
> Three.
> *(looking at Bud's card)*
> Queen.

*Fran hands the deck to Bud.*

> **BUD**
> Did you hear what I said, Miss Kubelik? I absolutely adore you.

> **FRAN**
> *(smiling)*
> Shut up and deal.

*Bud begins to deal, without taking his eyes off her, and with a look of pure joy on his face, deals . . . and deals . . . and keeps on dealing.*

# THE BLUES BROTHERS · 1980

**STARRING:**
JOHN BELUSHI / DAN AYKROYD
THE BLUES BROTHERS BAND / CAB CALLOWAY / JOHN CANDY

*Universal*

Screenplay by: DAN AYKROYD and JOHN LANDIS
Produced by: ROBERT K. WEISS
Directed by: JOHN LANDIS

INTERIOR: COUNTY CLERK'S OFFICE

**CLERK** (STEVEN SPIELBERG)
. . . and here is your receipt.

*Officers proceed to handcuff Jake* (JOHN BELUSHI) *and Elwood* (DAN AYKROYD) *as they stare into the rifles of the police.*

INTERIOR: JAIL CELLS

*A revue of the cast sings "Jailhouse Rock." As the crew sings, the cast in order of appearance appears on a roll credit.*

# CHARADE · 1963

**STARRING:**

CARY GRANT / AUDREY HEPBURN / WALTER MATTHAU
JAMES COBURN / GEORGE KENNEDY

*Universal*

Screenplay by: PETER STONE
Produced by: STANLEY DONEN
Directed by: STANLEY DONEN
Score by: HENRY MANCINI

INTERIOR: OFFICE – DAY

*Cruikshank* (CARY GRANT) *sits on the desk. Reggie* (AUDREY HEPBURN) *sits on a chair.*

**REGGIE**

. . . Marriage license. Did you say marriage license?

**CRUIKSHANK**

Don't change the subject. Just give me the stamps.

**REGGIE**

Oh, I love you, Adam . . . Alex . . . Peter . . . Brian . . . Whatever your name is. Oh, I love you. I hope we have a lot of boys and we can name them all after you.

**CRUIKSHANK**

But before we start that, may I have the stamps?

*They kiss.*

# CHINATOWN · 1974

**STARRING:**
JACK NICHOLSON / FAYE DUNAWAY / JOHN HUSTON
PERRY LOPEZ / JOHN HILLERMAN

*Paramount*

Screenplay by: ROBERT TOWNE
Produced by: ROBERT EVANS
Directed by: ROMAN POLANSKI

EXTERIOR: CHINATOWN

*Katherine* (BELINDA PALMER) *screams and is comforted by Noah Cross* (JOHN HUSTON).

> GITTES (JACK NICHOLSON)
> *(muttering)*
> Soon as possible . . .

> ESCOBAR (PERRY LOPEZ)
> What's that? What's that? You want to do your partner a big favor, you take him home. Take him home! Just get him the hell out of here. Go home, Jake.
> *(whispering)*
> I'm doing you a favor.

> WALSH (JOE MANTELL)
> and DUFFY (BRUCE GLOVER)
> Forget it, Jake. It's Chinatown!

> ESCOBAR
> *(to the Chinese gathering on the street)*
> All right. Come on, clear the area. On the sidewalk, get off the street.

*Sirens.*

# CITIZEN KANE · 1941

**STARRING:**

ORSON WELLES / JOSEPH COTTEN / EVERETT SLOANE
AGNES MOOREHEAD / DOROTHY COMINGORE

*RKO*

Screenplay by: HERMAN J. MANKIEWICZ ❦ and ORSON WELLES ❦
Produced by: ORSON WELLES
Directed by: ORSON WELLES

INTERIOR: THE KANE MANSION – EARLY EVENING

*Kane's possessions are crated.*

> **GIRL**
> If you could have found out what that Rosebud
> meant, I bet that would've explained everything.

> **THOMPSON** (WILLIARD ALLARD)
> No, I don't think so. No. Mister Kane was a man
> who got everything he wanted and then lost it.
> Maybe Rosebud . . . was something he couldn't
> get or something he lost. Anyway, it wouldn't
> have explained anything. I don't think any word
> can explain a man's life. No . . . I guess Rosebud
> is just a piece in a jigsaw puzzle—a missing
> piece. Well . . . come on everybody . . . we'll miss
> the train.

*Camera moves through the crated possessions of Charles Foster Kane.*

*A workman picks up the sled with the lettering* ROSEBUD. *He throws it into an incinerator. The flames consume the sled and the name* ROSEBUD.

EXTERIOR: THE KANE MANSION – DUSK

*Black smoke fills the sky. We then see a chain link fence with a sign:*
NO TRESPASSING
*Fade out on the crest "K" of the Kane estate.*

# CITY LIGHTS · 1931

**STARRING:**
CHARLIE CHAPLIN / VIRGINIA CHERRILL
HARRY MYERS / HANK MANN

*Charles Chaplin / UA*

Screenplay by: CHARLES CHAPLIN
Produced by: CHARLES CHAPLIN
Directed by: CHARLES CHAPLIN

EXTERIOR: THE FRONT OF THE FLOWER SHOP – DAY

*The blind girl* (VIRGINIA CHERRILL) *is seated holding a rose. She hands the tramp* (CHARLIE CHAPLIN) *the rose and touches his hand. She holds his hand as she realizes it is the tramp.*

**THE TRAMP (TITLE CARD)**

You? You can see now?

**BLIND GIRL (TITLE CARD)**

Yes, I can see now.

*A close-up of the tramp and the back of the blind girl's head is shown.*

# DRACULA · 1931

**STARRING:**

BELA LUGOSI / DAVID MANNERS / HELEN CHANDLER
DWIGHT FRYE / EDWARD VAN SLOAN

*Universal*

Written by: GARRETT FORD*
Produced by: CARL LAEMMLE, JR.
Directed by: TOD BROWNING, JR.

*Based on a play by Hamilton Deane and John Balderston,
and based on the novel by Bram Stoker.

INTERIOR: GOTHIC SUBTERRANEAN CHAMBERS – DAWN

> **MINA** (HELEN CHANDLER)
> Oh, John, John darling, I heard you calling but I
> couldn't say anything.

> **HARKER** (DAVID MANNERS)
> We thought he'd killed you, dear.

> **MINA**
> The daylight stopped him. Oh, if you could have
> seen the look on his face.

> **VAN HELSING** (EDWARD VAN SLOAN)
> There's nothing more to fear, Miss Mina.
> Dracula is dead forever. No, no, no. You must
> go.

> **MINA**
> But aren't you coming with us?

> **VAN HELSING**
> Not yet. Uh . . . presently. Come, John.

INTERIOR: LOWER CRYPT – VERY LONG SHOT

*The morning sunlight streams through the breaks in the walls as Harker
and Mina walk toward the top flight.*

# DR. EHRLICH'S MAGIC BULLET · 1940

**STARRING:**
EDWARD G. ROBINSON  /  RUTH GORDON  /  OTTO KRUGER
DONALD CRISP  /  MARIA OUSPENSKAYA

*Warner Bros.*

Screenplay by: JOHN HUSTON; HEINZ HERALD; NORMAN BURNSIDE
Produced by: WOLFGANG REINHARDT
Directed by: WILLIAM DIETERLE

INTERIOR: BEDROOM

*Ehrlich* (EDWARD G. ROBINSON) *is in bed, and two doctors are watching anxiously. Weakly, Ehrlich nods for his friends and associates to come closer to the bed; Hedi* (RUTH GORDON) *tries to arrange the pillows so that he will be more comfortable. He holds her hand as he speaks to his associates.*

> **EHRLICH**
> 606 works. We know. The magic bullet will serve
> thousands, and the principle upon which it works
> will serve against other diseases . . . many others,
> I think.
> *(pauses, weakness overcomes him, pats Hedi's hand)*
> Hedi, play a waltz, dear.

*Hedi exits.*

> **EHRLICH**
> In the days to come there will be epidemics of
> greed . . . hate . . . ignorance. We must fight
> them in life as we fought syphilis in the
> laboratory. We must fight . . . fight . . . fight. We
> must never stop fighting.

*As Ehrlich utters his last few words, his voice becomes weaker and weaker. His head sinks back on the pillow . . . and he dies. We see his profile for the last time. Silently, Hedi closes the bedroom door. The camera shifts to the title:* HIS MEMORY LIVES IN THE BODIES OF MEN—GLORIFIED AND MADE WHOLE.

# DUCK SOUP · 1933

**STARRING:**
GROUCHO MARX  /  HARPO MARX  /  CHICO MARX
ZEPPO MARX
MARGARET DUMONT  /  LOUIS CALHERN

*Paramount*

Screenplay by: BERT KALMAR, HARRY RUBY, ARTHUR SHEEKMAN,
NAT PERRIN
Produced by: LEO McCAREY
Directed by: LEO McCAREY

INTERIOR: FREEDONIA HEADQUARTERS

> **CHICOLINI** (CHICO MARX)
> Trentino!

> **FIREFLY** (GROUCHO MARX)
> Trentino, eh? Ahh! Call me an upstart, eh?

*Firefly is bombarded with fruit.*

> **TRENTINO** (LOUIS CALHERN)
> I surrender, I surrender!

> **FIREFLY**
> I'm sorry, you'll have to wait till the fruit runs out.

> **MRS. TEASDALE** (MARGARET DUMONT)
> *(sings)*
> Victory is ours! Hail, hail,
> Freedonia, land of the brave . . .

# E.T.—THE EXTRA-TERRESTRIAL ·
## (GROWING UP · A BOYS LIFE) · 1982

**STARRING:**
DEE WALLACE / HENRY THOMAS / PETER COYOTE
ROBERT MacNAUGHTON / DREW BARRYMORE
*Universal*
Screenplay by: MELISSA MATHISON
Produced by: STEVEN SPIELBERG; KATHLEEN KENNEDY
Directed by: STEVEN SPIELBERG

EXTERIOR: LANDING SITE – DUSK

**E.T.**

Be good.
*(looks up at Michael [*ROBERT MACNAUGHTON*], who
takes his hand)*
Thank you.
*(turns to Elliott [*HENRY THOMAS*])*
Come?

*Elliott looks up at the hovering spaceship. He turns to look at his brother,
sister (*DREW BARRYMORE*), mother (*DEE WALLACE*), Keys (*PETER COYOTE*),
and the boys, then looks back at E.T.*

**ELLIOTT**

Stay.

*They reach their arms out and embrace. Reluctantly they pull apart. E.T.
touches his chest where the heart-light has become a ruby glow illuminating
his and Elliott's face.*

**E.T.**

Ouch.

*Elliott takes E.T.'s forefinger and presses it to his own chest.*

**ELLIOTT**

Ouch!

*E.T. touches his finger lightly to Elliott's forehead.*

**E.T.**

I'll be right here.

*The door of the spaceship opens. E.T. notices the geranium on the ground,
lifts it and walks up the gangplank. Inside the doorway is a fellow creature
whose heart-light burns red. E.T. disappears into the ship; the gangplank
lifts; the door closes. The spaceship lifts into the air, leaving a vapor trail
like a rainbow. It moves quickly into the darkening sky, becoming smaller
until it is only a speck of white light: the first star of the evening.*

# THE GODFATHER · 1972 ▼

**STARRING:**

MARLON BRANDO ❘/ AL PACINO / JAMES CAAN
RICHARD CASTELLANO / JOHN CAZALE / DIANE KEATON

*Paramount*

Screenplay by: MARIO PUZO ❘ and FRANCIS FORD COPPOLA ❘ *
Produced by: FRANCIS FORD COPPOLA
Directed by: FRANCIS FORD COPPOLA

*\*Based on the novel by Mario Puzo.*

INTERIOR: THE DON'S OFFICE

> KAY (DIANE KEATON)

Is it true?

> MICHAEL (AL PACINO)

Don't ask me about my business.

> KAY

No!

> MICHAEL

All right. This one time . . . this one time . . . I'll
let you ask me about my affairs.

> KAY

Is it true?

> MICHAEL
> *(after a long pause)*

No.

*She throws her arms around him and hugs him. Then, she kisses him.*

> KAY
> *(through her tears)*

I think we both need a drink.

*Kay moves back into the kitchen to prepare drinks and sees Clemenza
(RICHARD CASTELLANO), Neri (RICHARD BRIGHT), and Rocco Lampone
enter the house with their bodyguard. She watches with curiosity as Michael
stands to receive them. He stands arrogantly, at ease, weight resting on one
foot slightly behind the other, one hand on his hip like a Roman emperor.
The capos stand before him.*

> CLEMENZA
> *(taking Michael's hand, kissing it)*

Don Corleone . . .

*The smile fades from Kay's face as they close the door.*

# GONE WITH THE WIND · 1939 ▼

**STARRING:**

CLARK GABLE / VIVIEN LEIGH ▮ / LESLIE HOWARD
OLIVIA DE HAVILLAND / THOMAS MITCHELL
HATTIE McDANIEL ▮

*M - G - M*

Screenplay by: SIDNEY HOWARD ▮ *
Produced by: DAVID O. SELZNICK
Directed by: VICTOR FLEMING ▮

*Based on the novel by Margaret Mitchell.*

CLOSE SHOT ON SCARLETT (VIVIEN LEIGH).

*She is stunned. She stands listening to the front door closing behind Rhett Butler (CLARK GABLE). She looks around, crushed by his words.*

> **SCARLETT**
> I can't let him go! There must be some way to bring him back!

*She walks around the room thinking, moving jerkily and without design, until suddenly she stops, as the camera moves up to her.*

> **SCARLETT**
> Oh I can't think about that now! I'll go crazy if I do! I'll think about it tomorrow. Tara, home. I'll go home and I'll think of some way to get him back! After all, tomorrow is another day!

# GOODBYE, MR. CHIPS · 1939

**STARRING:**

ROBERT DONAT ! / GREER GARSON / PAUL HENREID
TERRY KILBURN / JOHN MILLS

*M - G - M*

Screenplay by: R. C. SHERRIFF, CLAUDINE WEST, ERIC MASCHWITZ*
Produced by: VICTOR SAVILLE
Directed by: SAM WOOD
*Based on the novel by James Hilton.*

INTERIOR: BEDROOM

*Mr. Chips* (ROBERT DONAT) *is very ill. The old master lies in bed with his eyes closed. The music of the school song creeps in, then a distant voice singing softly.*

> **CHIPS**
> I thought I heard you saying it was a pity . . . a
> pity I never had . . . any children, eh? But you're
> wrong . . . I have . . . thousands of them . . .
> thousands of them . . . and all boys.

*He smiles. The music of the school song swells. A group of boys files past, tipping their hats and saying their names. As the last of the procession of students fades away, the figure of little Peter Colley* (TERRY KILBURN) *comes before us. He speaks straight into the camera and says in his youthful treble voice:*

> **COLLEY**
> Goodbye, Mr. Chips . . . Goodbye . . .

# GRAND HOTEL · 1932 ▼

**STARRING:**

GRETA GARBO / JOAN CRAWFORD / JOHN BARRYMORE
WALLACE BEERY / LIONEL BARRYMORE

*M - G - M*

Screenplay by: WILLIAM BLAKE*
Produced by: IRVING THALBERG
Directed by: EDMUND GOULDING

*Based on the novel by Vicki Baum.*

INTERIOR: LOBBY

> **SENF** (JEAN HERSHOLT)
> And your forwarding address?

> **KRINGELEIN** (LIONEL BARRYMORE)
> Eh, eh, the Grand Hotel in Paris.

> **FLAEMMCHEN** (JOAN CRAWFORD)
> How do you know there will be a Grand Hotel in
> Paris?

> **KRINGELEIN**
> Oh, oh, there's a Grand Hotel everywhere in the
> world.

> **DOCTOR** (LEWIS STONE)
> Good-bye, Mr. Kringelein.

> **KRINGELEIN**
> Oh, Doctor, good-bye, Doctor.

> **DOCTOR**
> Pain's gone already.

> **KRINGELEIN**
> Oh, pain. I have none, Doctor. Good-bye.

THE FRONT OF THE LOBBY OF THE GRAND HOTEL, FACING THE STREET –
DAY.

> **DOCTOR**
> The Grand Hotel. Always the same. People come,
> people go . . . nothing ever happens.

*Shot of the hotel's revolving door, turning but empty.*
   *Close-up of the name* Grand Hotel *on the side of arriving bus. The bus
driver's voice announces: "Grand Hotel!!"*

# THE GRAPES OF WRATH · 1940

**STARRING:**

HENRY FONDA / JANE DARWELL ! / JOHN CARRADINE
CHARLEY GRAPEWIN / DORRIS BOWDEN

*20th Century-Fox*

Screenplay by: NUNNALLY JOHNSON*
Produced by: NUNNALLY JOHNSON
Directed by: JOHN FORD !
*Based on the novel by John Steinbeck.*

INTERIOR: A TRUCK – DUSK

> MA (JANE DARWELL)
> We keep a-comin'. We're the people that live.
> They can't wipe us out. They can't lick us. We'll
> go on forever, Paw . . . cause . . . we're the
> people.

*The sound of an accordion is heard playing "Old Folks at Home."*

EXTERIOR: A ROW OF OLD JALOPIES, THEIR OWNERS' POSSESSIONS PILED
ON TOP, TRAVEL ONWARD.

# THE GREAT McGINTY · 1940

**STARRING:**

BRIAN DONLEVY / MURIEL ANGELUS / AKIM TAMIROFF
ALLYN JOSLYN / WILLIAM DEMAREST

*Paramount*

Screenplay by: PRESTON STURGES !
Produced by: PAUL JONES
Directed by: PRESTON STURGES

INTERIOR: CAFE

*McGinty* (BRIAN DONLEVY) *behind the bar. Boss* (AKIM TAMIROFF) *enters, grabs McGinty, swings him around. Confused voices offscreen.*

**BOSS**
So, I caught you again, you cheesy cheapskate!
Give me the dough!

**MCGINTY**
Listen, you fat little four-flusher . . .

**BOSS**

Fat!?

*They start to fight. Confused voices offscreen.*

**POLITICIAN**
*(offscreen)*
Come on—two bambas—
*(onscreen)*—
and quit horsing around!

*Crash offscreen.*

**POLITICIAN** (WILLIAM DEMAREST)
Time out, gents. Here we go again!

*Crash offscreen.*

# HAROLD AND MAUDE · 1971

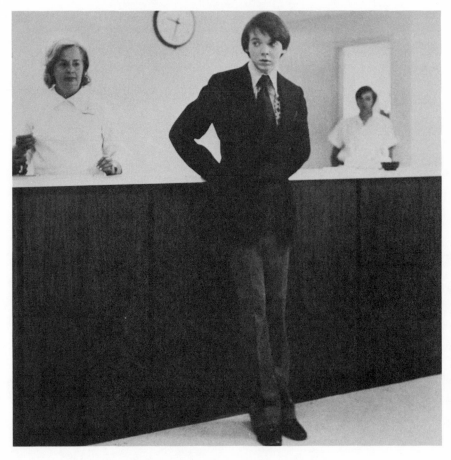

**STARRING:**

RUTH GORDON / BUD CORT / VIVIAN PICKLES
CYRIL CUSACK / CHARLES TYNER

*Paramount*

Screenplay by: COLIN HIGGINS
Produced by: COLIN HIGGINS
Directed by: HAL ASHBY

EXTERIOR: PROMONTORY – DAY

*The little hearse falls from the cliff, crashing at the bottom and bursting into flame.*

EXTERIOR: ON TOP OF THE CLIFF

*We look down at the burning vehicle. We hold and watch it burn.*

LONG SHOT

*Suddenly we hear the fumbled pickings of "Maude's Song" on a banjo. We pan up left and there is Harold, large as life.*

*He started slow but now he is gradually beginning to play the song in its original tempo. He gets better at it. We watch Harold amble down the road, strumming along, until he is only a small figure in the distance.*

# HIGH NOON · 1952

**STARRING:**

GARY COOPER / GRACE KELLY / LLOYD BRIDGES
THOMAS MITCHELL / KATY JURADO

*United Artists*

Screenplay by: CARL FOREMAN
Produced by: STANLEY KRAMER
Directed by: FRED ZINNEMANN

EXTERIOR: STREET – DAY

> **HENDERSON** (THOMAS MITCHELL)
> Soon as you walk through that door! Come on
> . . . I'll hold my fire . . .

*Henderson waits, holding Amy* (GRACE KELLY) *tightly. Wildly, she reaches up with her free hand and claws at his face and eyes. Kane* (GARY COOPER) *opens door and fires. Amy lands in the street, where Kane helps her up. They cling to each other.*

*People gather in the street. They look at Kane and Amy in silence.*

*Kane takes off his badge and drops it into the dust. Then slowly, without a backward glance, he and Amy ride out of town, the buckboard growing smaller in the background. The crowd remains silent as the buckboard passes out of view.*

# I AM A FUGITIVE FROM A CHAIN GANG · 1932

**STARRING:**

PAUL MUNI / GLENDA FARRELL / HELEN VINSON
PRESTON FOSTER / EDWARD ELLIS

*Warner Bros.*

Screenplay by: HOWARD J. GREEN, BROWN HOLMES, and SHERIDAN
GIBNEY*

Produced by: HAL B. WALLIS

Directed by: MERVYN LeROY

*Based on the novel by Robert E. Burns.*

EXTERIOR: ALLEY – NIGHT

*Allen* (PAUL MUNI) *stands in the dark shadows at the entrance to [an] alley. Helen* (HELEN VINSON) *stands watching, an expression of intense suffering and pity on her face. Allen, lost in the shadows of the night, is a broken and hunted animal.*

ALLEN

Forgive me, Helen . . . I had to take a chance to see you tonight. Just to say good-bye.

HELEN

Oh, dear! It was all going to be so different.

ALLEN

It is different. They've made it different. I've got to go!

HELEN

I can't let you go like this!

ALLEN

I've got to!

HELEN

Can't you tell me where you're going? Will you write?
*(he shakes his head)*
. . . But you must! How do you live?

ALLEN

I steal.

# IN THE HEAT OF THE NIGHT · 1967 ▼

**STARRING:**
SIDNEY POITIER / ROD STEIGER ❚ / WARREN OATES
LEE GRANT / SCOTT WILSON

*United Artists*

Screenplay by: STIRLING SILLIPHANT ❚
Produced by: WALTER MIRISCH
Directed by: NORMAN JEWISON

EXTERIOR: TRAIN STATION – DAY

*Tibbs (*SIDNEY POITIER*) and Gillespie (*ROD STEIGER*) stand beside a train. Tibbs takes his suitcase, which Gillespie was carrying.*

#### GILLESPIE
Thank you.

*Gillespie offers his hand, and they shake hands briefly.*

#### GILLESPIE
Bye-bye.

*Tibbs mounts the stairs of the train.*

#### GILLESPIE
Virgil?

*Tibbs looks back cautiously.*

#### GILLESPIE
You take care, you hear?

*A faint smile crosses Gillespie's face. Tibbs smiles in return, then winks.*

#### TIBBS
Yeah.

*Gillespie smiles broadly, considering something momentarily. He exits.*

*Ray Charles's voice is heard singing "In the Heat of the Night," as the train moves through the countryside.*

# IT'S A WONDERFUL LIFE · 1946

**STARRING:**

JAMES STEWART / DONNA REED / LIONEL BARRYMORE
THOMAS MITCHELL / HENRY TRAVERS

*RKO / Liberty*

Screenplay by: FRANCIS GOODRICH, ALBERT HACKETT,
FRANK CAPRA*
Additional scenes by: JO SWERLING
Produced by: FRANK CAPRA
Directed by: FRANK CAPRA
*Based on a story by Phillip Van Doren Stein.*

INTERIOR: LIVING ROOM

*Holding his daughter Zuzu* (KAROLYN GRIMES), *George* (JAMES STEWART) *glances down at a pile of money. His eye catches something on top of the pile. He recognizes it and reaches for it. It is Clarence's copy of* Tom Sawyer. *Zuzu opens it and George finds an inscription written in it.*

CLOSE UP: FLYLEAF OF BOOK

Dear George . . . Remember, <u>no</u> man is a failure who has friends. Thanks for the wings. Love, Clarence.

*Mary* (DONNA REED) *comes into shot.*

**MARY**

What's that?

**GEORGE**

That's a Christmas present from a very dear
friend of mine.

*Suddenly, a little bell on the Christmas tree begins to tinkle as it sways to and fro.*

**ZUZU**

Look, Daddy—
*(points to the bell)*
Teacher says every time a bell rings, an angel
gets his wings.

**GEORGE**

That's right, that's right. Atta boy, Clarence.

*The voices of people singing "Auld Lang Syne" swell into a final crescendo.*

# JAWS · 1975

**STARRING:**
ROY SCHEIDER / ROBERT SHAW / RICHARD DREYFUSS
LORRAINE GRAY / MURRAY HAMILTON

*Universal*

Screenplay by: PETER BENCHLEY and CARL GOTTLIEB*
Produced by: RICHARD ZANUCK and DAVID BROWN
Directed by: STEVEN SPIELBERG
Score by: JOHN WILLIAMS !
*Based on the novel by Peter Benchley.*

*The shark disappears into the deep, eventually slowed and stopped by the remnants of line still fastened by the bobbing barrels. Hooper (RICHARD DREYFUSS), on the surface, raises his mask, clears his eyes, and begins to kick toward Brody (ROY SCHEIDER). They are together, clinging to hunks of debris from the* Orca, *floating, shivering, and catching their breath.*
*A high wide angle shot shows the spot where the* Orca *went down, still roiling with bubbles. Debris litters the ocean. The two gather their resources for the long swim home. They chuckle.*

**HOOPER**

Quint?

**BRODY**

No.

*Brody and Hooper tread water.*

**BRODY**

We get in on those?

*Brody and Hooper paddle toward shore, using the boat's wreckage for support.*

**BRODY**

Hey, what day is this?

**HOOPER**

It's Wednesday. It's Tuesday, I think.

**BRODY**

Think the tide's with us?

**HOOPER**

Keep kickin'.

**BRODY**

I used to hate the water.

**HOOPER**

I can't imagine why.

*The camera shows a pristine, white sandy beach as the credits roll, while in the distance we see Brody and Hooper make for the shore.*

# THE JAZZ SINGER · 1927

**STARRING:**

AL JOLSON / MAY McAVOY / WARNER OLAND
EUGENIE BESSERER / OTTO LEDERER

Adaptation and continuity by: ALFRED A. COHN*
Produced by: WARNER BROS.
Directed by: ALAN CROSLAND

*Based on the play by Samson Raphaelson.*

TITLE CARD:
*The season passes—*
*and time heals—*
*the show goes on*

INTERIOR: THEATER – NIGHT

**JACK** (AL JOLSON)
*(singing)*

Mammy! I'm comin'!
I hope I didn't make you wait.
Mammy! I'm comin'!
Oh God I hope I'm not late.
Mammy, don't ya know me!
It's your little baby. I'd walk a million
miles for one of your smiles!
Mammy!

# KING KONG · 1933

**STARRING:**
ERNEST B. SCHOEDSACK / FAY WRAY
BRUCE CABOT / ROBERT ARMSTRONG / NOBLE JOHNSON

*RKO*

Screenplay by: JAMES CREELMAN and RUTH ROSE*
Produced by: MERIAN C. COOPER
Directed by: MERIAN C. COOPER

*Based on a story by Edgar Wallace.*

EXTERIOR: EMPIRE STATE BUILDING – FULL SHOT – DAWN

*A squadron of airplanes sweeps past King Kong with a roar of machine guns. He staggers, turns slowly and topples off the roof.*

EXTERIOR: EMPIRE STATE DOME – FULL SHOT – DAWN

> **DRISCOLL** (BRUCE CABOT)
> Ann, Ann, hang on, dear.

*Driscoll throws his arms about Ann* (FAY WRAY). *He holds her tight, protectively.*

EXTERIOR: STREET – FULL SHOT – DAWN

*Kong's head, blood trickling from his mouth. Denham emerges through the crowd.*

> **DENHAM**
> Let me through, officer, I'm Denham.

> **POLICEMAN**
> Just a moment. Oh, Lieutenant.

> **DENHAM**
> Lieutenant, I'm Carl Denham.

> **POLICEMAN**
> Well, Denham, the airplane got him.

> **DENHAM**
> Oh, no, it wasn't the airplane—it was beauty
> killed the beast.

# KING'S ROW · 1942

**STARRING:**

ANN SHERIDAN / ROBERT CUMMINGS / RONALD REAGAN
BETTY FIELD / CHARLES COBURN

*Warner Bros.*

Screenplay by: CASEY ROBINSON*
Produced by: DAVID LEWIS
Directed by: SAM WOOD

*Based on the novel by Henry Bellamann.*

INTERIOR: BEDROOM

*Randy* (ANN SHERIDAN) *hugs Drake* (RONALD REAGAN). *He holds her tight. He is grinning, laughing. (Music is "Invictus," sung by male chorus.)*

**DRAKE**
What was it you wanted, honey? To build a
house? We'll move into it in broad daylight. And
we'll invite the folks in, too. For Pete's sake, let's
give a party. I feel swell.

*Watching them, Parris* (ROBERT CUMMINGS) *backs out of the room and goes down the stairs, quickening his steps.*

EXTERIOR: MONAGHAN HOUSE

*Parris comes out the front door, hurries down the walk, through the gate. (The music continues throughout.)*

EXTERIOR: FRONT GATE AND DRIVEWAY, VON ELM PLACE – LONG SHOT TOWARD HOUSE

*The gate is open and Parris passes through. He lifts his face toward the house. Elise* (KARREN VERNE) *is standing on the terrace. She raises her arm straight above her head and waves, a gay, happy, childish gesture. She runs down the terrace steps on her way to meet him.*

*Parris quickens his step.*

# LITTLE CAESAR · 1930

**STARRING:**

EDWARD G. ROBINSON / DOUGLAS FAIRBANKS, JR.
GLENDA FARRELL / STANLEY FIELDS / SIDNEY BLACKMER

*Warner Bros.*

Screenplay by: FRANCIS EDWARDS FARAGON*
Adaptation by: ROBERT N. LEE
Produced by: WARNER BROS.
Directed by: MERVYN LeROY

*Based on a novel by W. R. Burnett.*

EXTERIOR: ALLEY

*Flaherty* (THOMAS JACKSON) *and others walk into scene. Rico* (EDWARD G. ROBINSON) *lies half sprawled, half propped up against a corner of the billboard.*

**FLAHERTY**

Well, Rico, it looks like you and I are going to
take that little ride together.

**RICO**

No, we ain't. I told you, little buzzard like you
will never put any cuffs on me.

**FLAHERTY**

You should have come out when I told you to,
Rico.

*Rico looks up at him defiantly. A spasm of pain racks his whole body. He is dying.*

**RICO**
*(gasps)*

Mother of Mercy—is this the end of Rico?

*Shot of poster reading* TIPSY TOPSY TURVY.

# THE MALTESE FALCON · 1941

**STARRING:**
HUMPHREY BOGART / MARY ASTOR / PETER LORRE
SYDNEY GREENSTREET / WARD BOND

*Warner Bros.*

Screenplay by: JOHN HUSTON*
Produced by: HENRY BLANKE
Directed by: JOHN HUSTON
*Based on the novel by Dashiell Hammett.*

INTERIOR: ROOM

*Sam Spade* (HUMPHREY BOGART) *and Police Inspector Polhaus* (WARD BOND) *are standing in front of the statue of a black bird.*

> **SPADE**
>
> Well, shall we be getting down to the hall?

> **POLHAUS**
> *(picks up statue)*
>
> It's heavy. What is it?

> **SPADE**
>
> The . . . er . . . stuff dreams are made of.

> **POLHAUS**
>
> Huh?

*Spade takes the statue from Polhaus's grasp and walks to the stairs, while Brigid O'Shaughnessy* (MARY ASTOR) *descends in the elevator with a police escort. The elevator door closes, and Spade walks down the stairs holding the black bird tightly.*

# NINOTCHKA · 1939

**STARRING:**

GRETA GARBO / MELVYN DOUGLAS / INA CLAIRE
BELA LUGOSI / SIG RUMAN

*M - G - M*

Screenplay by: CHARLES BRACKETT, BILLY WILDER, WALTER REISCH*
Produced by: ERNST LUBITSCH
Directed by: ERNST LUBITSCH

*Original story by Melchior Lenggel.*

INTERIOR: ROOM

**LEON** (MELVYN DOUGLAS)

I won't tell you what came between, I'll show
you. I'll prove it . . . but it will take a long time,
Ninotchka, at least a lifetime.

**NINOTCHKA** (GRETA GARBO)

Oh, but Leon, I'm only here for a few days.

**LEON**

All right, if you don't stay with me, then I'll have
to continue my fight. I'll travel wherever there
are Russian commissions. I'll turn them all into
Iranoffs, Buljanoffs, and Kopalskis. The world
will be crowded with Russian restaurants. I'll
depopulate Russia. Comrade, once you saved
your country by going back. This time you can
only save it by staying here.

**NINOTCHKA**

Well, if it's a choice between my personal interest
and the good of my country, how can I waver?
No one shall say Ninotchka was a bad Russian.

*Leon takes her in his arms. They kiss.*

**LEON**

Darling!

*Superimposed on the embrace we see a sign that reads* DINE WITH
BULJANOFF, IRANOFF & KOPALSKI.

*The camera pulls back to show people eating in front of the restaurant,
others walking past on the sidewalk. Kopalski* (ALEXANDER GRANACH) *is
picketing the place, wearing a sign that reads* BULJANOFF AND IRANOFF
UNFAIR TO KOPALSKI.

*He starts to turn around.* THE END *fades in and out.*

# NORTH BY NORTHWEST · 1959

**STARRING:**

CARY GRANT / EVA MARIE SAINT / JAMES MASON
LEO G. CARROLL / MARTIN LANDAU

*M - G - M*

Screenplay by: ERNEST LEHMAN
Produced by: ALFRED HITCHCOCK
Directed by: ALFRED HITCHCOCK

EXTERIOR: MOUNT RUSHMORE

*Close-up of Thornhill* (CARY GRANT) *looking down, his face drawn and tense.*

**THORNHILL**
*(with exertion)*

Here . . . reach . . . now . . .

**EVE** (EVA MARIE SAINT)
*(offscreen, gasping)*

I'm . . . trying . . .

**THORNHILL**

Come on . . . I've got you . . . up . . .

*Close-up of Eve looking up, her face showing intense physical strain.*

**EVE**

I can't make it . . .

**THORNHILL**
*(offscreen)*

Yes, you can . . . come on . . .

*Close-up of Thornhill.*

**THORNHILL**

Eve, harder . . . Come on, Mrs. Thornhill.

*As she lands beside him, we see that they are no longer on Mount Rushmore, but are side by side in the upper berth of a train's sleeper compartment.*

**EVE**

Ah, Roger, this is silly.

**THORNHILL**

I know, but I'm sentimental.

*He puts his arms around her, and as they kiss lovingly, the train is seen going into a tunnel.*

# THE ODD COUPLE · 1968

**STARRING:**

JACK LEMMON  /  WALTER MATTHAU

JOHN FIEDLER  /  HERB EDELMAN  /  MONICA EVANS

*Paramount*

Screenplay by: NEIL SIMON*
Produced by: HOWARD W. KOCH
Directed by: GENE SAKS
*Based on the play by Neil Simon.*

FULL SHOT – POKER TABLE

*The players look at Oscar* (WALTER MATTHAU) *with enormous pleasure.*

CLOSE-UP – OSCAR

OSCAR

> Well, whatta we gonna do? Are we gonna sit
> around, or are we gonna play poker?

FULL SHOT – POKER GROUP

ALL

> We're gonna play poker!

*General hubbub as they pass out the beer, deal the cards, and settle around
the table. Oscar sits.*

OSCAR

> Then let's play poker.

*He cleans the table as the players look at each other, all stifling a chuckle.
He picks up a butt.*

OSCAR

> Hey, and boys, boys, boys! Let's watch the
> cigarette butts, shall we? This is my house, not a
> pigsty!

*They play.*

# THE PHILADELPHIA STORY · 1940

**STARRING:**

CARY GRANT / KATHARINE HEPBURN / JAMES STEWART ❢
RUTH HUSSEY / JOHN HOWARD

*M - G - M*

Screenplay by: DONALD OGDEN STEWART ❢ *
Produced by: JOSEPH L. MANKIEWICZ
Directed by: GEORGE CUKOR

*\*Based on the play by Phillip Barry.*

INTERIOR: ALTAR IN LIVING ROOM

> **DINAH** (VIRGINIA WIEDLER)
> *(ecstatically)*
> I did it! I did it all!

> **UNCLE WILLIE** (ROLAND YOUNG)
> I have the feeling I've been through all this
> before—in another life.

*He looks as a figure squeezes in behind him. It is Sidney Kidd (HENRY DANIELL). Kidd smiles sweetly at Uncle Willie, and takes a miniature camera out of his pocket. Focusing carefully on the group at the altar, he leans forward to take the picture. The camera clicks.*

CLOSE SHOT – AT ALTAR

*At the click of the camera, Liz (RUTH HUSSEY), Tracy (KATHARINE HEPBURN), Dexter (CARY GRANT), and Mike (JAMES STEWART) all whirl simultaneously to glare in the direction of the click.*

INSERT – *SPY* MAGAZINE

*All four of them in exactly the same pose as the previous scene, glaring from the pages of* Spy *Magazine.*

INSERT – *SPY* MAGAZINE

*Dexter and Tracy kiss at the close of the ceremony.*

# A PLACE IN THE SUN · 1951

**STARRING:**

MONTGOMERY CLIFT  /  ELIZABETH TAYLOR  /  SHELLEY WINTERS
KEEFE BRASSELLE  /  RAYMOND BURR

*Paramount*

Screenplay by: HARRY BROWN and MICHAEL WILSON **!**
Produced by: GEORGE STEVENS
Directed by: GEORGE STEVENS **!**
*Based on the novel* An American Tragedy *by Theodore Dreiser.*

INTERIOR: PRISON CORRIDOR – CLOCK ON WALL READS 5:00 A.M.

*Prayers are heard as the warden walks down the prison corridor. The warden stops in front of George's* (MONTGOMERY CLIFT) *cell.*

> **WARDEN**
> *(quietly)*
> You'll have to go now, son. Come on, son.

*They move out of the cell, a guard taking his place at George's left, the chaplain at his right, and the warden with the second guard behind. They walk slowly through an open door into the corridor of the last mile. Camera follows. On either side of the corridor are the cells of other condemned men. As the procession passes each cell, we hear the prisoners' muffled farewells:*

> **VOICE**
> So long, kid.

> **VOICE**
> I hope you find a better world than this.

> **VOICE**
> Good-bye, George, I'll be seeing you.

*Through a series of dissolves we see George's face. He is walking down the corridor but he is mentally far away, lost in his memory of embracing Angela Vickers* (ELIZABETH TAYLOR). THE END *is seen over George's face as he thinks of Angela.*

# THE PRESIDENT'S ANALYST · 1967

**STARRING:**

JAMES COBURN / GODFREY CAMBRIDGE
SEVERN DARDEN / JOAN DELANEY / PAT HARRINGTON

*Paramount*

Screenplay by: THEODORE J. FLICKER
Produced by: STANLEY RUBIN
Directed by: THEODORE J. FLICKER

*Apparently Kropotkin* (SEVERN DARDEN) *has been away for a while. The front door opens. Sidney* (JAMES COBURN), *happy, tired, delighted to see his wife, his friends, his cozy home. They sit with drinks in front of the fire.*

**KROPOTKIN**

From Russia with love. Caviar . . . beluga, champagne, Lithuanian. Well . . .

**DON** (GODFREY CAMBRIDGE)

Congratulations!

**SIDNEY**

For what?

**DON**

It was in my evening report. He's now a major-general.

**SIDNEY**

Oh.

**KROPOTKIN**

But there is one thing you do not know. I caught my father dealing with Red China! I am now the head of the foreign section.

**DON**

Sensational!

*(to Sidney)*

So how come he's getting healthier than me?

**SIDNEY**

I think it's time we considered group therapy.

**KROPOTKIN**

Let's get drunk! . . . Joy to the world!

# RAIDERS OF THE LOST ARK · 1981

**STARRING:**

HARRISON FORD / KAREN ALLEN / WOLF KAHLER
PAUL FREEMAN / RONALD LACEY

*Paramount*

Screenplay by: LAWRENCE KASDAN
Story by: GEORGE LUCAS
Produced by: FRANK MARSHALL
Directed by: STEVEN SPIELBERG

EXTERIOR: PENTAGON STEPS – DAY

*Indy* (HARRISON FORD) *emerges from the building.*

> **MARION** (KAREN ALLEN)
> Hey! What happened? You don't look very happy.

> **INDY**
> Fools! Bureaucratic fools!

> **MARION**
> What did they say?

> **INDY**
> They don't know what they've got there.

> **MARION**
> Well, I know what I've got here.
> *(smiles)*
> C'mon. Buy you a drink. You know, a drink.

*They move down the steps together, smiling.*

INTERIOR: GOVERNMENT WAREHOUSE

*The Ark of the Covenant sits in a wooden crate. A wooden lid comes down and hides it from view. The lid is solidly nailed to the crate as we read the stenciled message on top:* TOP SECRET, ARMY INTELLIGENCE #9906753. DO NOT OPEN. *The hammering is completed and hands shift the heavy crate onto a dolly.*

# REBECCA · 1940 ▼

**STARRING:**
LAURENCE OLIVIER / JOAN FONTAINE
GEORGE SANDERS / JUDITH ANDERSON / NIGEL BRUCE
*Selznick International Pictures*
Screenplay by: ROBERT E. SHERWOOD and JOAN HARRISON*
Produced by: DAVID O. SELZNICK
Directed by: ALFRED HITCHCOCK
*Based on the novel by Daphne du Maurier.

*In the background, flames rise higher around Manderley. Suddenly Mrs. de Winter* (JOAN FONTAINE) *sees Maxim* (LAURENCE OLIVIER) *and an instant later they are in each other's arms.*

**MAXIM**

Are you all right, darling?

**MRS. DE WINTER**

Oh, yes. I'm all right.

**MAXIM**
*(kissing her, holding her tightly)*

Are you all right?

**MRS. DE WINTER**

But Mrs. Danvers—she's gone mad! She said she'd rather destroy Manderley than see us happy here.

*All of a sudden there is a cry: "Look, the West Wing!" At the window of the West Wing the figure of Mrs. Danvers* (JUDITH ANDERSON) *can be seen, seemingly undisturbed by the fire. There is a triumphant, defiant look on her face as the flames shoot up and about her.*

*Suddenly, without warning, the ceiling collapses in Rebecca's bedroom.*

*The last thing we see is the nightcase on Rebecca's bed. As the flames gradually creep up and start to devour the initial R on the case, we fade out.*

# THE ROARING TWENTIES · (THE WORLD MOVES ON)
## 1939

**STARRING:**

JAMES CAGNEY / PRISCILLA LANE / HUMPHREY BOGART
GLADYS GEORGE / JEFFREY LYNN

*Warner Bros.*

Screenplay by: JERRY WALD, RICHARD MACAULAY, ROBERT ROSSEN
Story by: MARK HELLINGER
Produced by: HAL B. WALLIS and SAM BISCHOFF
Directed by: RAOUL WALSH

EXTERIOR: ON THE STAIRS

**PANAMA** (GLADYS GEORGE)

He's dead!

**POLICEMAN**
*(to Panama)*

Who is this guy?
*(pulls out book and pencil)*

**PANAMA**
*(slowly)*

This is Eddie Bartlett.

**POLICEMAN**

How were you hooked up with him?

**PANAMA**
*(slowly; it becomes increasingly difficult for her to
talk)*

I could never figure it out.

*The policeman looks at her strangely; she turns her head away.*

**POLICEMAN**

What was his business?

**PANAMA**
*(her voice choked with emotion, tears streaming down
her cheeks)*

He used to be a big shot.

# ROCKY · 1976 ▼

**STARRING:**
SYLVESTER STALLONE / TALIA SHIRE
BURT YOUNG / CARL WEATHERS / BURGESS MEREDITH

*United Artists*

Screenplay by: SYLVESTER STALLONE
Produced by: ROBERT CHARTOFF and IRWIN WINKLER
Directed by: JOHN G. AVILDSEN ▮

INTERIOR: ARENA OF A BOXING RING

*A bruised Rocky* (SYLVESTER STALLONE) *frantically looks in all directions and barely manages to see Adrian* (TALIA SHIRE) *jumping up and down, waving. Amid the confusion, he repeatedly calls her name.*

**ROCKY**

Adrian! Adrian! Adrian!

*Adrian works her way through the crowd into the ring and finally they embrace.*

**ADRIAN**

I love you.

**ROCKY**

I love you.

**ADRIAN**

I love you. I love you. I love you . . .

# ROSEMARY'S BABY · 1968

**STARRING:**

MIA FARROW / JOHN CASSAVETES / RUTH GORDON !
SIDNEY BLACKMER / MAURICE EVANS

Screenplay by: ROMAN POLANSKI*
Produced by: WILLIAM CASTLE
Directed by: ROMAN POLANSKI

*Based on the novel by Ira Levin.

INTERIOR: ROOM

*Laura-Louise* (PATSY KELLY) *comes forward, making a face at Rosemary* (MIA FARROW) *as she passes her.*

**ROMAN** (SIDNEY BLACKMER)
Rock him.

**ROSEMARY**
You're trying to get me to be his mother.

**ROMAN**
Aren't you his mother?

*The baby is crying. Rosemary walks slowly to the bassinet which Roman has been rocking.*

*Guy* (JOHN CASSAVETES) *and Sapirstein* (RALPH BELLAMY) *pass Minnie* (RUTH GORDON). *As Sapirstein starts forward, Minnie moves to him, motioning for silence.*

*The assembled company gathers around the bassinet. The Japanese man snaps a picture. The baby gurgles. Rosemary rocks the bassinet, leans over it, then straightens up. The camera pans to window. A woman's voice sings "La, La, La . . ." Our last image is an aerial shot moving back from the Bramford.*

# SERGEANT YORK · 1941

**STARRING:**

GARY COOPER / WALTER BRENNAN / JOAN LESLIE
GEORGE TOBIAS / STANLEY RIDGES

*Warner Bros.*

Screenplay by: ABEN FINKEL, HARRY CHANDLER, JOHN HUSTON,
HOWARD KOCH
Produced by: JESSE L. LASKY
Directed by: HOWARD HAWKS

FULL SHOT: THE LAND – DAY

*Alvin* (GARY COOPER) *blinks his eyes and grunts, as though he had received a body blow. He shoots a look at Gracie* (JOAN LESLIE).

> **GRACIE**
> *(studiedly casual)*
> It's yours, Alvin . . .

*Alvin hears but it's several moments before the words penetrate. When they do, he turns to her, stunned.*

> **GRACIE**
> It's all yours, Alvin. They give it to you . . . the people of the state of Tennessee . . . for what you done.

> **ALVIN**
> *(stammers, almost speechless)*
> You mean . . . ?

> **GRACIE**
> *(her eyes brilliant)*
> Only it's two hundred acres . . . and the house is bigger with more winders . . . and the kitchen's got a pump. And it's for us.

*Alvin stands dumbly, shaking his head. His eyes travel over the whole length and breadth of the farm, drinking it all in.*

> **ALVIN**
> The Lord shore does move in mysterious ways.

> **GRACIE**
> C'mon.

*They walk toward the house.*

# SHANE · 1953

**STARRING:**
ALAN LADD / JEAN ARTHUR / VAN HEFLIN
(WALTER) JACK PALANCE / BRANDON DE WILDE

*Paramount*

Screenplay by: A. B. GUTHRIE, JR., and JACK SHER*
Produced by: GEORGE STEVENS
Directed by: GEORGE STEVENS
*Based on the novel by Jack Schaefer.*

EXTERIOR: GRAFTON'S – DAY

*Shane* (ALAN LADD) *unties his horse, mounts it, turns away from Joe* (BRANDON DE WILDE). *Puzzled, Joe watches him for a moment. Shane rides off, and returns, after seeing Joe following him.*

> **SHANE**
> Bye, little Joe.

> **JOE**
> He'd never have even cleared the holster, would he, Shane? . . . Pa's got a lot of things for you to do, and Mother wants you. I know she does. . . . Shane! Shane!

*Shane heels his horse and rides away. Joe stares after him. As Shane's figure loses itself in the darkness, Joe begins to cry for Shane to come back, as we see Shane ride over a mountain.*

# THE SHOP AROUND THE CORNER · 1940

**STARRING:**

MARGARET SULLAVAN / JAMES STEWART
FRANK MORGAN / JOSEPH SCHILDKRAUT / SARA HADEN

*M - G - M*

Screenplay by: SAMSON RAPHAELSON*
Produced by: ERNST LUBITSCH
Directed by: ERNST LUBITSCH
*Based on the play by Miklos Laszlo.*

INTERIOR: SHOP

> **KLARA** (MARGARET SULLAVAN)
> Why, I called you bowlegged!

> **KRALIK** (JAMES STEWART)
> *(laughing it off)*
> Yes, and I wanted to prove that I wasn't. I was
> going to go out on the street and pull up my
> trousers.

> **KLARA**
> Yes . . . well . . . would you mind very much if I
> asked you to pull them up now?

*Kralik steps back and pulls up his trousers to the knees, proving forever that he is not bowlegged. With a sigh of relief, Klara goes to him and they embrace.*

# SINGIN' IN THE RAIN · 1952

**STARRING:**
GENE KELLY / DEBBIE REYNOLDS / DONALD O'CONNOR
JEAN HAGEN / CYD CHARISSE

*M - G - M*

Screenplay by: BETTY COMDEN and ADOLPH GREEN
Produced by: ARTHUR FREED
Directed by: GENE KELLY and STANLEY DONEN

INTERIOR: GRAUMAN'S CHINESE THEATER

*The orchestra goes into the song with Lina (JEAN HAGEN) apparently singing. But behind the curtain we see Kathy (DEBBIE REYNOLDS) singing into the microphone. The lip-synching is perfect. Suddenly, Don (GENE KELLY), Cosmos (DONALD O'CONNOR), and Simpson (MILLARD MITCHELL) pull the curtain. Lina is mouthing away and making flapping gestures. The crowd starts laughing. Kathy, truly bewildered, looks around and suddenly runs down the steps of the stage to the audience and begins rushing up the aisle to escape. Don runs out on the stage.*

**DON**

Ladies and gentlemen! Stop that girl!

*There are ad libs from the audience.*

**DON**

That girl running up the aisle . . . stop her!
That's the girl whose voice you heard and loved
tonight. She's the real star of the picture. Kathy
Selden!

*The audience applauds. Kathy is stopped in the aisle and turns toward Don. Don starts to sing "You Are My Lucky Star." There are tears in Kathy's eyes as Don comes down the steps and reaches out for her.*

*The scene dissolves into an outdoor sunlit scene showing a huge billboard with Don's picture facing a picture of Kathy. The two of them are standing below and looking up at the billboard, which reads:*

### SINGIN' IN THE RAIN
### DON LOCKWOOD     KATHY SELDEN
### MONUMENTAL PICTURES

*The song, sung by an offscreen chorus, reaches a soaring finish.*

# SOME LIKE IT HOT · 1959

**STARRING:**
JACK LEMMON / TONY CURTIS / MARILYN MONROE
JOE E. BROWN / GEORGE RAFT

*United Artists*

Screenplay by: BILLY WILDER and I.A.L. DIAMOND
Produced by: BILLY WILDER
Directed by: BILLY WILDER

EXTERIOR: JERRY (JACK LEMMON) AND OSGOOD (JOE E. BROWN)
IN SPEEDBOAT

*Jerry looks at Osgood, who is grinning from ear to ear. He claps his hands
to his forehead. How is he going to get himself out of this?*

> **JERRY**
> *(in a woman's voice)*
> And I have a terrible past. For three years now
> I've been living with a saxophone player.

> **OSGOOD**
> I forgive you.

> **JERRY**
> *(with growing desperation)*
> I can never have children.

> **OSGOOD**
> We can adopt some.

> **JERRY**
> Well, you don't understand, Osgood!
> *(rips off wig and uses a male voice)*
> I'm a man!

> **OSGOOD**
> Well—nobody's perfect.

# STAGECOACH · 1939

### STARRING:

**JOHN WAYNE / CLAIRE TREVOR / THOMAS MITCHELL !**
**LOUISE PLATT / ANDY DEVINE**

*United Artists*

Screenplay by: DUDLEY NICHOLS*
Produced by: WALTER WANGER
Directed by: JOHN FORD
*Based on the story "Stage to Lordsburg" by Ernest Haycox.*

EXTERIOR: OUTSIDE OF SALOON

> CURLY (GEORGE BANCROFT) and DOC BOONE
> (THOMAS MITCHELL)
> *(to horses)*

Hiya, hiya . . .

*The horses leap away. In a few seconds, the buckboard with Ringo (JOHN WAYNE) and Dallas (CLAIRE TREVOR) is out of sight and even the sound of the runaway horses is growing faint. Doc and Curly laugh.*

> DOC

Well, they're saved from the blessings of civilization.

> CURLY

Yeah.
> *(laughs)*

Doc . . . I'll buy ya' a drink.

> DOC

Just one.
> *(more laughs)*

*The scene dissolves to a view of the moving buckboard. Darkness still lies over the land, but sunrise whitens the clouds on the horizon as the buckboard comes up in silhouette against it. Then the vehicle wheels away into the sunrise, carrying Ringo and Dallas to their new life.*

# STAR WARS · (THE ADVENTURES OF LUKE SKYWALKER) · 1977

**STARRING:**
MARK HAMILL / HARRISON FORD / CARRIE FISHER
PETER CUSHING / ALEC GUINNESS

*20th Century-Fox*

Screenplay by: GEORGE LUCAS
Produced by: GARY KURTZ
Directed by: GEORGE LUCAS

INTERIOR: MAIN HANGAR

> **LUKE** (MARK HAMILL)
> I knew you could do it!

> **HAN** (HARRISON FORD)
> Well, I wasn't going to let you get all the credit
> and take all the reward.

*Leia* (CARRIE FISHER) *hugs Luke and he spins her around; she goes over to Han. She grabs him, hugging him and laughing.*

> **LEIA**
> And you . . . I knew it was more to you than
> money.

> **LUKE**
> Oh, no. R2? Can you hear me? Say something.

> **C-3PO** (ANTHONY DANIELS)
> You can repair him, can't you?

> **REPAIRMAN**
> We'll get to work on him right away.

> **C-3PO**
> Sir, you must repair him . . . if any of my circuits
> or gears will help, I'll gladly donate them.

> **LUKE**
> He'll be all right.

INTERIOR: MAIN THRONE ROOM

*Luke, C-3PO, Han, and Chewbacca* (PETER MAYHEW) *enter the ruins of the main temple. Hundreds of troops are lined up in neat rows, banners are flying, and at the far end stands a vision in white—the beautiful young Senator Leia. Luke and the others solemnly march up the aisle and kneel before her. After Leia places a gold medallion around Han's neck, they turn and face the assembled troops, who bow before them.*

# SULLIVAN'S TRAVELS · 1941

**STARRING:**
JOEL McCREA / VERONICA LAKE / ROBERT WARWICK
WILLIAM DEMAREST / ERIC BLORE

*Universal*

Screenplay by: PRESTON STURGES
Produced by: PAUL JONES
Directed by: PRESTON STURGES

INTERIOR: AIRPLANE

> **MR. HADRIAN** (PORTER HALL)
> *(gently)*
> Why don't you want to make *Oh Brother, Where Art Thou?*, Sully?

> **SULLIVAN** (JOEL McCREA)
> Well, in the first place, I'm too happy to make *Oh Brother, Where Art Thou?*
> *(looks at the girl [VERONICA LAKE])*
> In the second place, I haven't suffered enough to make *Oh Brother, Where Art Thou?*

> **MR. HADRIAN**
> You haven't suffered enough?

> **MR. LEBRAND** (RAYMOND WALBURN)
> He hasn't suffered enough.

*His listeners look at each other goggle-eyed.*

> **MR. LEBRAND**
> *(despairingly, picking up the book)*
> But, Sully . . .

> **SULLIVAN**
> *(gently)*
> I'll tell you something else: there's a lot to be said for making people laugh . . . did you know that's all some people have? It isn't much . . . but it's better than nothing in this cockeyed caravan . . .
> *(shakes his head reminiscently)*
> Boy!

*The girl looks up at him and chuckles. We hear the echo of laughter, and superimposed on the screen are the images of the people he has met throughout his travels.*

# SUNSET BOULEVARD · (CAN OF BEANS) · 1950

**STARRING:**

GLORIA SWANSON / WILLIAM HOLDEN / ERICH VON STROHEIM
FRED CLARK / JACK WEBB

*Paramount*

Screenplay by: BILLY WILDER ❘, CHARLES BRACKETT ❘,
D. M. MARSHMAN, JR. ❘
Produced by: CHARLES BRACKETT
Directed by: BILLY WILDER

INTERIOR: TO MOVIE CAMERA

*Norma Desmond* (GLORIA SWANSON) *arranges the scarf around her shoulders and proudly descends the staircase. The camera grinds. At the foot of the stairs, she stops.*

### NORMA

I can't go on with the scene. I'm too happy. Do you mind, Mr. DeMille, if I say a few words? Thank you. I just want to tell you all how happy I am to be back in the studio making a picture again. You don't know how much I've missed all of you. And I promise you I'll never desert you again, because after *Salome* we'll make another picture, and another picture. You see, this is my life. It always will be. There's nothing else . . . just us and the cameras and those wonderful people out there in the dark.

*(coming toward camera)*

All right, Mr. DeMille, I'm ready for my close-up.

# THE THIN MAN · 1934

**STARRING:**
WILLIAM POWELL / MYRNA LOY / MAUREEN O'SULLIVAN
NAT PENDLETON / MINNA GOMBELL

*M - G - M*

Screenplay by: ALBERT HACKETT and FRANCES GOODRICH*
Produced by: HUNT STROMBERG
Directed by: W. S. VAN DYKE

*Based on the novel by Dashiell Hammett.*

INTERIOR: TRAIN – NIGHT

*Nick* (WILLIAM POWELL) *and Nora* (MYRNA LOY) *are inside their private compartment. Nora seats herself on the lower bunk.*

**NORA**

Nicky, put Asta in here with me tonight.

**NICK**
*(laughs)*

Oh, yeah?

*Nick tosses Asta up to the top bunk. The musical theme, "California, Here I Come," is heard. Asta covers his eyes with his paw.*

# TRADING PLACES · 1983

**STARRING:**
DAN AYKROYD / EDDIE MURPHY
RALPH BELLAMY / DON AMECHE / DENHOLM ELLIOTT

*Paramount*

Screenplay by: TIM HARRIS and HERSCHEL WEINGROD
Produced by: ROBERT K. WEISS
Directed by: JOHN LANDIS

EXTERIOR: THE VILLA NEXT DOOR

*On the veranda, Louis Winthrope* (DAN AYKROYD) *and Ophelia* (JAMIE LEE CURTIS) *are being served a champagne brunch by a host of servants. Louis peers down over the deck at Billy Ray* (EDDIE MURPHY) *and lifts his glass in a toast.*

**LOUIS**

Looking good, Billy Ray!

*Billy Ray turns and glances up at Winthrope, raising his glass in return.*

**BILLY RAY**

Feeling good, Louis!

*Louis and Billy Ray smile at one another, and drink deeply.*

# THE TREASURE OF THE SIERRA MADRE
## 1948

**STARRING:**
HUMPHREY BOGART / WALTER HUSTON !
TIM HOLT / BRUCE BENNETT / BARTON MacLANE

*Warner Bros. First National*

Screenplay by: JOHN HUSTON ! *
Produced by: HENRY BLANKE
Directed by: JOHN HUSTON !
*Based on the novel by B. Traven.*

EXTERIOR: PLAZA IN MEXICO – DAY

*Curtain* (TIM HOLT) *and Howard* (WALTER HUSTON) *mount their horses.*

**HOWARD**

Good luck.

**CURTAIN**

Same to you.

*Howard's Indian companions ride off with him. Curtain watches them ride away. Howard turns and waves at him; Curtain waves back, and then he, too, leaves.*

*We see something blowing along the road. It is the canvas sack once owned by Dobbs* (HUMPHREY BOGART), *now torn and empty.*

# THE UNTOUCHABLES · 1987

**STARRING:**
KEVIN COSTNER / SEAN CONNERY !
CHARLES MARTIN SMITH
ANDY GARCIA / ROBERT DE NIRO

*Paramount*

Screenplay by: DAVID MAMET
Produced by: ART LINSON
Directed by: BRIAN DE PALMA

## EXTERIOR: POLICE HEADQUARTERS – DAY

*Ness* (KEVIN COSTNER) *walks out of police headquarters. On the sidewalk is the scoop who followed Ness to the raid at the warehouse.*

> **SCOOP**
> Mr. Ness . . . Mr. Ness, any comments for the record . . . ?

*Ness shakes his head.*

> **SCOOP**
> The man who put Al Capone on the spot!

> **NESS**
> I just happened to be there when the wheel went around . . .

*Ness starts to move past him. The reporter stops him.*

> **SCOOP**
> They say they're going to repeal Prohibition. What will you do then?

*Beat. Ness smiles.*

> **NESS**
> I think I'll have a drink.

*Ness moves past the reporter, down the street.*

# WEST SIDE STORY · 1961 ❚

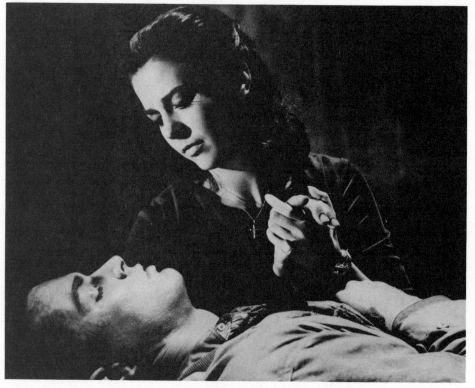

**STARRING:**
NATALIE WOOD / RICHARD BEYMER / GEORGE CHAKIRIS ❚
RITA MORENO ❚/ RUSS TAMBLYN

*Mirisch Pictures*

Screenplay by: ERNEST LEHMAN*
Produced by: ROBERT WISE
Directed by: ROBERT WISE ❚ and JEROME ROBBINS ❚
*Based on the musical play* West Side Story.
*Book by:* ARTHUR LAURENTS
*Music by:* LEONARD BERNSTEIN
*Lyrics by:* STEPHEN SONDHEIM

*Maria* (NATALIE WOOD) *leans low over Tony's* (RICHARD BEYMER) *face.*

**MARIA**

Te adoro, Anton.

*She kisses him gently. Music starts as two Jets and two Sharks lift up Tony's body. One of his legs falls; Pepe* (JAY NORMAN) *quickly steps forward to add his support, and the boys start to carry him out of the playground. Some of the others, boys and girls, fall in behind to make a procession, as Baby John* (ELIOT FELD) *picks up Maria's shawl and places it over her head.*

*Maria sits quietly, like a woman in mourning, as the music builds and the procession moves on. At last she gets up and, despite the tears on her face, lifts her head and turns to follow Tony's body being borne off by Jets and Sharks. The adults—Doc* (NED GLASS), *Schrank* (SIMON OAKLAND), *Krupke* (WILLIAM BRAMLEY)—*stand watching, bowed, alone. And nearby, looking across at each other uneasily, and then moving off in opposite directions, are the four Jets and Sharks who have not joined the procession, who are not yet ready, perhaps never will be ready, to give up war as a way of life.*

# WHITE HEAT · 1949

**STARRING:**

JAMES CAGNEY / VIRGINIA MAYO / EDMUND O'BRIEN
MARGARET WYCHERLY / STEVE COCHRAN

*Warner Bros.*

Screenplay by: IVAN GOFF and BEN ROBERTS*
Produced by: LOUIS F. EDELMAN
Directed by: RAOUL WALSH
*Based on a story by Virginia Kellogg.*

EXTERIOR: TOP OF THE HORTON SPHERE – NIGHT

*Another bullet tears into Cody's (JAMES CAGNEY) chest. He staggers, laughing, despite the pain. He realizes he's through. Suddenly, the gas is ignited from the blast of Cody's gun and he is in front of a raging fire. Below, Fallon (EDMUND O'BRIEN), Evans (JOHN ARCHER), and others run from the flaming area.*

> **CODY**
> Made it Ma . . . top of the world!

*There is a huge explosion, completely enveloping Cody. The men stare at the raging fire in silence.*

ON GROUND

> **EVANS**
> Cody Jarrett!

> **FALLON**
> He finally got to the top of the world and it blew up right in his face!

# THE WIZARD OF OZ · 1939

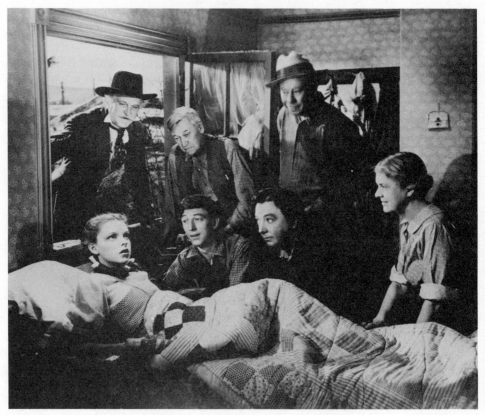

**STARRING:**

JUDY GARLAND / RAY BOLGER / BERT LAHR
JACK HALEY / FRANK MORGAN

*M - G - M*

Screenplay by: NOEL LANGLY, FLORENCE RYDERSON,
EDGAR ALLEN WOOLF*
Produced by: MERVYN LeROY
Directed by: VICTOR FLEMING
*Based on the novel by L. Frank Baum

INTERIOR: ROOM

*Dorothy* (JUDY GARLAND) *sits in the bed with Auntie Em* (CLAIR BLANDICK) *near her. The professor* (FRANK MORGAN) *looks in the window. Uncle Henry* (CHARLEY GRAPEWIN), *Hunk* (RAY BOLGER), *Hickory* (JACK HALEY), *Zeke* (BERT LAHR) *are gathered around. Toto jumps up on the bed and Dorothy hugs him.*

**DOROTHY**
Doesn't anybody believe me?

**UNCLE HENRY**
Of course we believe you, Dorothy

**DOROTHY**
Oh, but anyway, Toto, we're home! Home! And
this is my room . . . and you're all here! And I'm
not going to leave here ever, ever again, because
I love you all! And . . . Oh, Auntie Em, there's
no place like home!

# YANKEE DOODLE DANDY · 1942

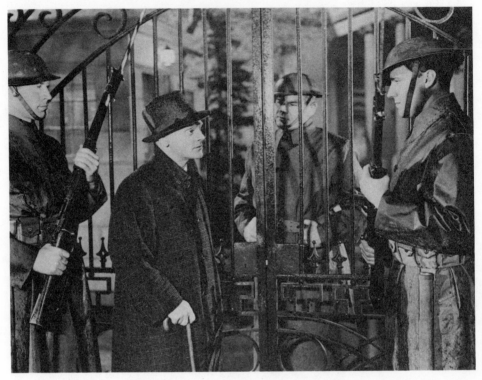

**STARRING:**
JAMES CAGNEY **!** / JOAN LESLIE
WALTER HUSTON / IRENE MANNING / ROSEMARY DECAMP

*Warner Bros.*

Screenplay by: ROBERT BUCKNER, EDMUND JOSEPH, JULIUS J. and
PHILIP G. EPSTEIN*
Produced by: HAL B. WALLIS
Directed by: MICHAEL CURTIZ
Lyrics and music by: GEORGE M. COHAN
*Story by Robert Buckner.*

EXTERIOR: STREET OUTSIDE THE WHITE HOUSE

*A company of soldiers is parading by. As they march they are singing "Over There." The people on the sidewalk cheer them and join in the song. As the music fills the air, we see George (*JAMES CAGNEY*) coming out of the White House grounds. As he sees and hears the soldiers singing his song he stops short. He is so greatly affected that all he can do is stand and look. A soldier marching past him is singing. He turns to George.*

**SOLDIER**
*(to George)*

What's the matter, old-timer, don't you remember this song?

**GEORGE**
*(smiling strangely)*

Seems to me I do.

**SOLDIER**

Well, I don't hear anything.

*George starts to sing with the soldiers. Singing, he unconsciously starts down the street in step with the soldiers. The words grow very loud and distinct . . . "And we won't come back till it's over, over there!"*

# · VINTAGE BOOKS ON FILM ·

*A Man for All Seasons* by Robert Bolt ($8.00, 0-679-72822-8)
*The Sheltering Sky* by Paul Bowles ($11.00, 0-679-72979-8)
*Mildred Pierce* by James M. Cain ($8.95, 0-679-72321-8)
*The Postman Always Rings Twice* by James M. Cain ($8.00, 0-679-72325-0)
*O Pioneers!* by Willa Cather ($9.00, 0-679-74362-6)
*The Big Sleep* by Raymond Chandler ($9.00, 0-394-75828-5)
*Farewell, My Lovely* by Raymond Chandler ($10.00, 0-394-75827-7)
*The Lady in the Lake* by Raymond Chandler ($10.00, 0-394-75825-0)
*A Tale of Two Cities* by Charles Dickens ($7.95, 0-679-72965-8)
*Babette's Feast* by Isak Dinesen ($6.00, 0-394-75929-X)
*Out of Africa & Shadows on the Grass* by Isak Dinesen ($12.00, 0-679-72475-3)
*The Book of Daniel* by E.L. Doctorow ($10.00, 0-679-73657-3)
*Ragtime* by E.L. Doctorow ($10.00, 0-679-73626-3)
*The Commitments* by Roddy Doyle ($8.00, 0-679-72174-6)
*Madame Bovary* by Gustave Flaubert ($10.00, 0-679-73636-0)
*September September* (the basis for *Memphis*) by Shelby Foote
    ($9.00, 0-679-73543-7)
*Howards End* by E. M. Forster ($10.00, 0-679-72255-6)
*A Room With a View* by E. M. Forster ($9.00, 0-679-72476-1)
*Where Angels Fear to Tread* by E. M. Forster ($9.00, 0-679-73634-4)
*A Gathering of Old Men* by Ernest J. Gaines ($10.00, 0-679-73890-8)
*Wild at Heart* by Barry Gifford ($8.95, 0-679-73439-2)
*Shoot the Piano Player* by David Goodis ($7.95, 0-679-73254-3)
*The Tin Drum* by Günter Grass ($15.00, 0-679-72575-X)
*Claudius the God* by Robert Graves ($14.00, 0-679-72573-3)
*I, Claudius* by Robert Graves ($11.00, 0-679-72477-X)
*Monster in a Box* by Spalding Gray ($9.00, 0-679-73739-1)
*The Maltese Falcon* by Dashiell Hammett ($9.00, 0-679-72264-5)
*The Thin Man* by Dashiell Hammett ($9.00, 0-679-72263-7)
*A Rage in Harlem* by Chester Himes ($8.00, 0-679-72040-5)
*Gideon's Trumpet* by Anthony Lewis ($10.00, 0-679-72312-9)

*Common Ground* by Anthony Lukas ($15.00, 0-394-74616-3)

*Death in Venice & Other Stories* by Thomas Mann ($10.00, 0-679-72206-8)

*At Play in the Fields of the Lord* by Peter Matthiessen ($11.00, 0-679-73741-3)

*Bright Lights, Big City* by Jay McInerney ($9.00, 0-394-72641-3)

*Moby-Dick* by Herman Melville ($12.50, 0-679-72525-3)

*Lolita* by Vladimir Nabokov ($9.00, 0-679-72316-1)

*Shattered* by Richard Neely ($9.00, 0-679-73498-8)

*Swann's Way* by Marcel Proust ($13.00, 0-679-72009-X)

*Kiss of the Spider Woman* by Manuel Puig ($11.00, 0-679-72449-4)

*Jazz Cleopatra* by Phyllis Rose ($14.00, 0-679-73133-4)

*Cyrano de Bergerac* by Edmond Rostand ($9.95, 0-679-73413-9)

*Iron & Silk* by Mark Salzman ($10.00, 0-394-75511-1)

*Dr. Jekyll and Mr. Hyde* by Robert Louis Stevenson ($7.00, 0-679-73476-7)

*Sophie's Choice* by William Styron ($13.00, 0-679-73637-9)

*After Dark, My Sweet* by Jim Thompson ($7.95, 0-679-73247-0)

*The Grifters* by Jim Thompson ($8.95, 0-679-73248-9)

*The Player* by Michael Tolkin ($10.00, 0-679-72254-8)

*Life on the Mississippi* by Mark Twain ($10.50, 0-679-72527-X)

*The Adventures of Tom Sawyer* by Mark Twain ($8.50, 0-679-73501-1)

*Birdy* by William Wharton ($10.00, 0-679-73412-0)

*The Hot Spot* by Charles Williams ($8.95, 0-679-73329-9)


SCREENPLAYS

*Hannah and Her Sisters* by Woody Allen ($10.00, 0-394-74749-6)

*Three Films by Woody Allen: Broadway Danny Rose, Zelig, The Purple Rose of Cairo* ($16.00, 0-394-75304-6)